Nadia Comaneci
Biography

The Inspiring Story of one

Gymnastics Legend

Frank L. Robinson

TABLE OF CONTENTS

INTRODUCTION

On July 18, 1976, in Montreal, Canada, a young gymnast from Romania stepped onto the Olympic stage and did something the world had never seen before. Nadia Comăneci, just 14 years old, performed a flawless routine on the uneven bars. As she dismounted and landed perfectly, the crowd held its breath. Moments later, the scoreboard lit up with a score no one expected: 1.00. Confused murmurs rippled through the arena. Was it a mistake? It wasn't. The scoreboard couldn't display a 10.00—a perfect score. No one had ever achieved it before. But Nadia had. She had made history, becoming the first gymnast to score a perfect ten at the Olympics. This moment would change gymnastics forever. Before Nadia's performance, the sport was known for its grace and beauty, but only some thought perfection was possible. Her flawless routine proved otherwise. She didn't just raise the bar; she redefined it. Suddenly, young gymnasts worldwide had a new dream—not just to compete, but to be perfect, just like Nadia. Nadia's perfect ten was more than just a score—it symbolized what could be achieved through hard work, determination, and courage. She became an instant hero, not only in Romania but across the globe. Newspapers and television broadcasts told her story, and her image appeared on magazine covers everywhere. People marvelled at how someone so young could perform with confidence and skill. But what made Nadia truly special was not just her talent. She is determined to keep improving, even after making history. She continued to compete, winning five Olympic gold medals and becoming one of the most decorated gymnasts in history. Her performances inspired a generation of young athletes to believe perfection was possible if they worked hard and never gave up. Even today, Nadia Comăneci's name is synonymous with excellence in gymnastics. Her story teaches us that reaching for perfection isn't about being flawless all the time. It's about believing in yourself, pushing past obstacles, and striving to be your best. Nadia's journey began with one perfect 10, but it didn't end there. She used that moment as a stepping stone to achieve even greater things—and to inspire the world to dream big.

CHAPTER 1: A CHILDHOOD IN ROMANIA

Discovering Gymnastics

Nadia Comăneci was born on November 12, 1961, in a small town called Onești, Romania. From the beginning, it was clear that Nadia was full of energy. As a young girl, she loved running, climbing trees, and jumping around. She was always moving, and her parents, Ștefan and Maria, often wondered how she could have so much energy daily. Little did they know, this energy would one day help her become one of the greatest gymnasts the world had ever seen.

Growing up in Romania during the 1960s, life was simple. Nadia lived in a modest home with her parents and her younger brother, Adrian. The family didn't have many luxuries, but they had love and support for one another. Nadia spent most of her days playing outside with her friends, enjoying the fresh air and the freedom to explore One day, when Nadia was about six years old, something happened that changed her life forever. During recess at school, she and her friends played on the playground. They were doing flips, handstands, and cartwheels just for fun. Nadia's movements were quick, smooth, and full of confidence. She had a natural talent for these activities, even though she had never practised them. Not far away, a gymnastics coach named Bela Karolyi was visiting the school. He and his wife, Marta, were looking for young children with potential to join their gymnastics program. Bela noticed Nadia right away. She stood out from the other kids because of her fearless attitude and the way she moved so effortlessly. It was as if gymnastics came naturally to her. After watching her for a while, Bela approached Nadia's teacher and asked to meet her parents. He believed Nadia had the talent to become a great gymnast, but he knew it would take hard work and dedication. When Bela met with Ștefan and Maria, he explained that Nadia had a special gift. He invited them to bring her to his gymnastics training centre in Onești. At first, Nadia's parents were unsure. Gymnastics was not a common sport in their town, and they didn't know much about it. But they could see how much Nadia enjoyed moving and flipping around. They also noticed how excited she was about learning something new. After talking it over, they decided to give it a try. Nadia's first day at the gym was unforgettable. The training centre was filled with equipment she had never seen before—balance beams, uneven bars, and mats for tumbling. It was like a new world, and Nadia couldn't wait to explore it. Bela and Marta welcomed her warmly and began teaching her the basics of gymnastics. At first, some of the exercises were challenging. Nadia had to learn how to balance on the beam, swing on the bars, and perfect her landings. But she didn't give up. Every day, she practised with determination and focus. What amazed her coaches most was her fearless spirit. Nadia was fearless in trying new skills, even if they seemed complicated. Within a few weeks, Nadia's progress was remarkable. She quickly learned the routines and techniques that other children took months to master. Bela and Marta were impressed by how fast she improved. They could see that Nadia was talented, hardworking, and determined to succeed. Gymnastics soon became Nadia's favourite activity. She loved the feeling of flying through the air and the excitement of learning new skills. Every time she mastered a new move, she felt a sense of pride and joy. Her parents noticed how happy she was and supported her every step of the way. As Nadia continued to train, she dreamed of competing in gymnastics competitions. She wanted to show others what she could do and see how far her talent could take her. Bela and Marta encouraged her to aim high, telling her that she could achieve great things with hard work and dedication. For Nadia, discovering gymnastics was like finding a new home. The gym became a place where she could express herself, push her limits, and discover her capabilities. It began a journey that would take her to heights she never imagined.

Early Training with Coach Bela Karolyi

She was excited when Nadia Comăneci first walked into the gymnastics training centre in Onești. Everything was new—the equipment, the routines, and the feeling of being in a place where gymnastics was taken seriously. But meeting her coach, Bela Karolyit, made the biggest difference in Nadia's journey. Bela was a passionate and determined coach who believed that young gymnasts could achieve greatness with the proper guidance and hard work. Bela Karolyi had a keen eye for spotting talent, and from the moment he saw Nadia, he knew she had something special. Her natural grace, fearless attitude, and determination set her apart from other children. But talent alone wasn't enough to become a champion. Bela understood that Nadia would need discipline, focus, and hours of practice to reach her full potential. Nadia's training began with the basics. Bela and his wife, Marta, taught her to stretch properly and warm up before each practice. This was important to prevent injuries and prepare her body for the challenging routines ahead. Nadia quickly learned that gymnastics wasn't just about having fun—it required precision, strength, and flexibility. One of the first skills Nadia worked on was balancing on the beam. At first, walking steadily on such a narrow surface seemed almost impossible. But with Bela's guidance and encouragement, Nadia practised repeatedly. She learned to focus her mind, keep her body steady, and trust her instincts. Before long, she was not only walking on the beam but also performing small jumps and turns with confidence. Another essential part of her training was learning to swing on the uneven bars. Nadia loved the feeling of flying through the air as she moved from one bar to the other. Bela taught her to grip the bars tightly, swing with momentum, and land safely. It wasn't easy, and there were times when Nadia slipped or fell. But each time, she got back up and tried again, determined to improve. Bela's ability to push his gymnasts while supporting them made him an exceptional coach. He believed in Nadia's potential and set high expectations for her. He often reminded her that hard work and perseverance were the keys to success. Nadia took those words to heart and gave her best effort in every practice. As the weeks turned into months, Nadia's progress was impressive. She began mastering more advanced skills, such as tumbling routines and complex jumps. Bela and Marta were amazed by how quickly she improved. Nadia's determination and love for gymnastics made her a joy to coach. The training was sometimes challenging. There were long days when Nadia felt tired or frustrated, especially when learning a new skill took longer than expected. But Bela taught her the importance of patience and persistence. He explained that every gymnast, no matter how talented, faces challenges. What mattered most was not giving up. Nadia's parents, Ștefan and Maria, watched with pride as their daughter grew more robust and more confident. They could see how much she loved gymnastics and how hard she worked to improve. They supported her by ensuring she had the time and energy to focus on her training. Bela also emphasized the importance of teamwork and respect. Although gymnastics is often seen as an individual sport, Nadia trained alongside other young gymnasts. Bela encouraged them to support and cheer for one another, creating a positive and motivating environment. Nadia made many friends at the gym, and they pushed each other to improve. Under Bela's guidance, Nadia began competing in local gymnastics competitions. These early experiences taught her how to perform under pressure and stay focused in front of an audience. Each competition was a chance to showcase what she had learned and gain valuable experience. Nadia's success in these competitions didn't go unnoticed. Bela and Marta saw that she had the potential to compete at a national level and even represent Romania in international events. They continued challenging her with more difficult routines, knowing she could achieve great things. For Nadia, training with Bela Karolyi was more than just learning gymnastics—it was the beginning of a journey that would shape her future. His guidance, encouragement, and belief in her abilities helped her grow into a determined and fearless athlete.

CHAPTER 2: THE RISE TO FAME

National Competitions

As Nadia Comăneci grew more robust and more skilled under the guidance of Bela and Marta Karolyi, her love for gymnastics only deepened. The once-energetic little girl who played on the school playground was now a dedicated athlete, ready to show her talents on a bigger stage. Nadia's training had been intense and focused, and it wasn't long before she began competing in national competitions across Romania. These events were crucial in shaping her path toward

becoming a world-renowned
gymnast. In Romania, gymnastics
was a respected sport, but it was
challenging to stand out. Many
talented young athletes competed,
each one hoping to catch the
attention of judges and coaches.
For Nadia, entering her first
national competition was both
exciting and nerve-wracking. She
had trained for months, perfecting
her routines and working tirelessly
on every detail. Still, the thought
of performing in front of judges, a
crowd, and her peers brought
butterflies to her stomach. Her
first national competition took
place in a gymnasium filled with
spectators. The air buzzed with

excitement as gymnasts prepared to showcase their skills. Nadia stood quietly, waiting for her turn. Her coach, Bela, reminded her to stay calm and focused. "Remember," he said reassuringly, "you've practised this routine many times. Trust yourself." When Nadia's name was called, she took a deep breath and stepped onto the mat. Her first event was the balance beam, a narrow surface where even the slightest wobble could cost points. As she climbed onto the beam, the crowd fell silent. Nadia focused her mind, blocking out the noise and distractions around her. With grace and precision, she moved through her routine—each step, jump and turn executed flawlessly. Her dismount was perfect, and she landed firmly on both feet, earning applause from the audience. Next came the uneven bars, an event that had become one of Nadia's favourites. She loved swinging high and moving smoothly from one bar to the other. Her routine was challenging, but she had practised it countless times in the gym. Her movements were fluid and controlled as she performed, impressing the judges with her skill and confidence. By the end of the competition, Nadia had captured everyone's attention in the arena. Her talent impressed the judges and earned high scores in every event. When the final results were announced, Nadia had placed among the top competitors. It was a proud moment for her, her family, and her coaches. Bela and Marta knew that this was just the beginning of something extraordinary.

Earning a Spot on the Olympic Team

After Nadia Comăneci's remarkable performance at the national competitions, the next challenge was far more significant: earning a spot on Romania's Olympic gymnastics team. Many young gymnasts shared this dream, but only a few ever had the chance to make it a reality. For Nadia, the road to the Olympics was about demonstrating her skills and proving she had the mental toughness to compete on the world stage. In the early 1970s, Romania's gymnastics program was rapidly growing in stature, and the Olympic Games were considered the ultimate goal for every gymnast. The 1976 Summer Olympics in Montreal, Canada, were just around the corner, and the Romanian gymnastics team was eager to secure their place in the competition. As the Olympics approached, the pressure to succeed intensified. For Nadia, every practice, every competition, and every moment spent training with her coach, Bela Karolyi, became more crucial than ever before. Bela Karolyi, who had been instrumental in Nadia's development, knew that the Olympics were within reach for her. However, the selection process was rigorous, and only the best gymnasts from Romania would be chosen to represent the country. Nadia had already shown her potential in national competitions, but the selection trials for the Olympic team were a completely different challenge. To earn a spot on the Olympic team, Nadia had to prove herself against some of the best gymnasts in Romania. The trials were held at a major competition, where gymnasts would perform their routines before the most experienced judges and coaches. It was a tense and highly competitive event, and every gymnast knew the stakes were high. There were no second chances—only one opportunity to impress the judges and secure a spot. Nadia was nervous as she prepared for the trials. But she also knew that she had been working tirelessly for this moment. Her training with Bela had been intense. From perfecting her routines to strengthening her body and mind, she was ready to give it her all. She recalled Bela's words of encouragement: "You have everything it takes to succeed. Just trust yourself." The day of the trials arrived, and Nadia entered the gymnasium filled with anticipation. The crowd buzzed with excitement, and the air was thick with the pressure of competition. One by one, the gymnasts performed their routines. Nadia was calm and focused, determined not to let the pressure get to her. Her first event was the balance beam. As she stepped onto the narrow beam, the entire room seemed to hold its breath. Nadia moved gracefully and confidently, executing each element of her routine precisely. The judges were watching closely, but Nadia didn't let that distract her. She focused entirely on the task, performing every skill with control and poise. The routine was flawless, and when she dismounted, the audience applauded. It was clear that Nadia had given it her best. Next, Nadia moved on to the uneven bars, an equipment she had always enjoyed. She soared through her routine, swinging effortlessly from one bar to the next. Every move was sharp, and her transitions between elements were smooth and seamless. She landed the dismount perfectly, and the judges' scores reflected the difficulty and skill she demonstrated. Throughout the competition, Nadia continued to impress. Her floor exercise, where she showed off her athleticism and flexibility, was a crowd favourite. She performed with energy and excitement, earning high marks from the judges. Nadia was at the top of her game, performing each routine with the confidence of a seasoned champion. As the trials came to a close, the judges tallied the scores. Many talented gymnasts competed, but it was clear that Nadia stood out. When the results were announced, her

name was called as one of the
gymnasts chosen for the Romanian
Olympic team. The joy and
excitement Nadia felt at that
moment were indescribable. She
had worked so hard for this, and
now her dream of competing in the
Olympics was coming true. This
moment was a turning point in
Nadia's life. Her selection to the
Olympic team marked the
beginning of a new chapter in her
gymnastics career. She was no
longer just a rising star in
Romania—she was now part of a
team that would represent her
country on the world stage. But as
exciting as it was, Nadia knew the
journey ahead would be even more

challenging. Nadia's spot on the Olympic team resulted from years of dedication and hard work. She had proven herself at the national level, and now she had earned her place among the best gymnasts in the world. The Olympic Games in Montreal would be the ultimate test of her skills, strength, and determination.

CHAPTER 3: THE 1976 MONTREAL OLYMPICS

The Journey to Montreal

The road to the 1976 Montreal Olympics was long and challenging for Nadia Comăneci. It wasn't just about the hours of practice and dedication—it was about the dream of performing on the world's biggest stage. For Nadia, a gymnast from Romania, the Olympics were the ultimate goal. And now, after years of hard work and sacrifice, she was finally on the verge of making that dream a reality. Nadia's journey began with the rigorous selection process in Romania, where she earned her spot on the national gymnastics team. Once that was secured, the next step was the long, exciting road to Montreal. However, it wasn't just about the journey from one place to another. It was about mentally and physically preparing for the challenge of representing her country on the global stage. The journey to Montreal wasn't a short one. Nadia, her teammates, and their coaches had to travel a long distance from Romania to Canada. The team boarded a plane, and as they flew through the skies, Nadia couldn't help but think about the significance of this trip. This was more than just another competition—it was the Olympics, a once-in-a-lifetime opportunity to make history. She had worked hard to get here; now it was time to show the world what she could do. During the flight, Nadia remembered the many years of training, beginning in her hometown of Gheorgheni, where she first discovered her love for gymnastics. She remembered the long hours in the gym, the early mornings, and the constant support and encouragement from her coach, Bela Karolyi. As the plane soared toward Montreal, all the hard work she had put in seemed to come together. The moment she had been waiting for was approaching. When the team finally arrived in Montreal, the excitement was palpable. The city was buzzing with energy as athletes from all over the world came for the Olympic Games. For Nadia, everything felt more significant than she had imagined. The crowds, the media attention, and the other athletes—it was overwhelming, yet thrilling. The atmosphere was unlike anything she had ever experienced. The team was taken to their training facility and began preparing for the upcoming gymnastics events. Nadia's days were filled with practice, but she also had to adjust to the pressure of competing on

such a grand stage. The stakes
were high, and everyone wanted to
perform at their best. But despite
the excitement and pressure,
Nadia knew she had to stay
focused. She had come this far,
and there was no turning back
now. As the days passed, Nadia
practised her routines with her
usual dedication. She perfected
every movement, from the precise
jumps on the balance beam to the
smooth swings on the uneven bars.
Bela, her coach, oversaw her,
offering advice and
encouragement. The team worked
together to support each other,
helping one another perfect their
routines. Nadia was determined to

give her best performance ever, knowing she had the chance to make history. But it wasn't just the gymnastics skills that Nadia had to focus on. The pressure of competing on such a big stage was immense, with millions of eyes watching. It was a new experience for her, requiring much mental preparation. Nadia's coach, Bela, worked closely with her to help her stay calm and composed. He reminded her to trust her abilities and not let the pressure get to her. It was crucial that Nadia kept a clear mind and focused on her routines, one move at a time. Finally, after days of preparation, the moment Nadia had been waiting for arrived. It was time to step onto the Olympic stage. Nadia stood at the edge of the competition floor, watching the other gymnasts perform their routines. The crowd cheered, and the energy in the arena was electric. Nadia felt excited, but she kept her nerves under control. She had dreamed of this moment for so long; now it was her turn. The journey to Montreal had been long and challenging, but it had all led to this moment. Nadia knew this was her chance to show the world what she could do. The gymnastics world had its eyes on her, and she was ready to take the stage and make history.

Making History with a Perfect 10

The atmosphere in the Olympic Gymnastics Hall in Montreal was electric as the gymnastics competition began. Nadia Comăneci, a gymnast from Romania, stood backstage, her heart racing. She had worked tirelessly for this moment, and now the time had come to step into the spotlight. But this competition was even more special because it wasn't just any gymnastics meet—it was the Olympics. And for Nadia, it was her chance to make history. The moment she stepped onto the floor, Nadia knew this was the opportunity she had been waiting for her entire life. She had prepared for months, even years, and had come far from the young girl practising in Romania. As she stood at the edge of the balance beam, staring out at the thousands of spectators, she took a deep breath. The nerves were still there, but Nadia had trained herself to stay calm and focused. This was her time. Nadia's first event was the balance beam, and it was here that she would make history. As she moved onto the narrow beam, the crowd fell silent, knowing they were about to witness something extraordinary. With grace and poise, Nadia began her routine. Her every move was precise—her

jumps, turns, and even the
slightest movements were
executed flawlessly. She
performed each element of her
routine with such confidence that
it was as if she were in complete
control of the beam itself. And
then, at the moment when most
gymnasts would hope for just a
solid performance, Nadia did
something that no one had ever
seen before. She completed a
perfect routine. Every movement
was so precise that it seemed
impossible to improve. The judges
sat in awe, and when the scores
flashed on the board, it was clear
that something incredible had just
happened. Nadia's balance beam

routine score was 10.00, the first perfect 10 in Olympic gymnastics history. The crowd erupted into applause, but for Nadia, everything went still for a moment. A perfect 10—an achievement that no gymnast had ever reached in the Olympics. It was a moment of pure excellence and would go down in history. But for Nadia, it wasn't just about the score. It was about proving to herself and the world that she had what it took to be great. As she moved on to her following events, Nadia's confidence soared. She had already made history with that perfect score, but it still needed to be done. Her next challenge was

the uneven bars, where she had
always excelled. As she swung
through the air, her movements
were fluid and controlled. Every
transition was seamless, and when
she dismounted perfectly, the
crowd erupted in cheer. Nadia
knew she had performed well, but
she also knew that her earlier
perfect ten would make all eyes on
her even more focused.
Throughout the rest of the
competition, Nadia continued to
impress. Her floor routine was
filled with energy and grace, and
as she completed her vault, it was
clear that she had become a
favourite for the gold medal. But it
was not just her stunning

performances that were impressive—it was the fact that, at just 14 years old, Nadia was performing like a seasoned veteran. She had already earned the respect of everyone in the arena, but her true legacy was beginning. After each event, the scores continued to be high, and Nadia's performances were praised by the judges and commentators alike. But what truly stood out was her ability to stay calm and focused throughout it all. The pressure of competing on the world's biggest stage could have easily overwhelmed a young gymnast, but Nadia rose to the challenge. She showed the world that gymnastics was about physical ability and mental strength. By the end of the competition, Nadia had made history not just once but multiple times. She had earned three perfect 10s in her performances, a feat that had never been achieved before. Nadia's score of 10.00 on the balance beam, followed by a flawless performance on the uneven bars and another perfect score on the floor exercise, was enough to secure her the gold medal in all-around gymnastics. She had won the hearts of fans worldwide and forever changed the history of Olympic gymnastics. Nadia Comăneci's perfect 10s were not just numbers—they represented the dedication, passion, and tireless effort she had put into her sport. But most of all, her perfect scores showed the world that anything was possible. Nadia's achievements in Montreal were a turning point in gymnastics history, inspiring countless young gymnasts to pursue excellence and never give up on their dreams. For Nadia, the perfect 10 culminated years of hard work. It was a reward for every early morning, every problematic practice, and every sacrifice she had made. While the perfect 10s were a testament to her exceptional skill, they also reflected the incredible journey

that had brought her to the
Olympic Games. Nadia Comăneci
was no longer just a gymnast from
Romania—she was a global icon, a
symbol of dedication,
perseverance, and the pursuit of
perfection. As the final medals
were awarded, Nadia stood atop
the podium, holding her gold
medal high. She had made history,
but more importantly, she had
shown the world that nothing was
impossible if you worked hard
enough and believed in yourself.
The young gymnast from Romania
had forever changed the sport of
gymnastics and had inspired
generations of athletes to come.

CHAPTER 4: LIFE AS A YOUNG CHAMPION

Dealing with Fame at a Young Age

Nadia Comăneci's life changed forever after the 1976 Montreal Olympics. She became an international sensation when she scored the first perfect 10 in Olympic gymnastics history. At just 14 years old, Nadia had won multiple Olympic gold medals and made history like no gymnast before her. But with this incredible success came a new challenge—handling fame at such a young age. Nadia's world was suddenly filled with attention from every direction. The media couldn't get enough of her. Newspapers, magazines, and television stations worldwide wanted to interview her, take her picture, and share her story with their audiences. Nadia went from being a gymnast training in a gym in Romania to being the most famous athlete on the planet. Everywhere she went, people recognized her. It was overwhelming. For Nadia, dealing with fame was a huge adjustment. Before the Olympics, she had been a typical teenager—training hard, spending time with her family, and enjoying life as a young gymnast. But now, she was constantly in the

spotlight. It wasn't just the
Olympic Games that had brought
her fame; it was the perfect 10s
and her gold medals. The world
was watching her, and Nadia had
to figure out how to balance being
a teenager and a global superstar.
One of the biggest challenges
Nadia faced was the loss of her
privacy. She could no longer walk
down the street without being
recognized. People wanted to take
pictures with her or ask for her
autograph wherever she went. She
was no longer just Nadia, the
young gymnast from
Romania—she was a symbol of
excellence, and that came with a
lot of attention. Nadia learned

quickly that fame meant constant attention from the public. But, with the attention came the pressure to maintain her image. People expected perfection from her—not just in gymnastics, but in everything she did. This pressure was especially difficult for a young girl who had just entered her teenage years. Nadia had worked her whole life for this moment, but the reality of fame was not what she had imagined. Instead of focusing solely on gymnastics, she had to deal with interviews, media appearances, and fan expectations. For someone so young, it was a lot to handle. Nadia didn't have the luxury of being a typical teenager who could go out with friends or relax without worrying about public opinion. The press scrutinized everything she did. Despite these challenges, Nadia handled the situation with grace and maturity. She relied heavily on the support of her family and coach, Bela Karolyi, to help her stay grounded. Her parents were there for her every step of the way, reminding her of who she was before the fame and keeping her focused on the goals she had set for herself. Bela, too, played an essential role in helping her manage the pressures of being in the spotlight. He was not just a coach but a mentor who helped

Nadia stay focused on gymnastics, keeping her mind on her training rather than the distractions that came with fame. But even with the support of those closest to her, Nadia was still just a young girl trying to navigate a world that was now much bigger than she had ever imagined. Her world-stage success meant she had to travel frequently for competitions and promotional events. These trips took her away from home, making it difficult to have a sense of normalcy. She was constantly in a new country, meeting new people, and facing the pressure of representing her country and her sport at the highest level. At the same time, Nadia was still a teenager trying to figure out who she was outside of gymnastics. Like any young person, she wanted to experience the world in ways that didn't involve competing. But fame made that problematic. She couldn't just go to a mall or a park with her friends like other teenagers could. Instead, her life was a whirlwind of interviews, photoshoots, and public appearances. The public's expectations were high, and Nadia had to learn how to cope. One of the most challenging aspects of being famous at such a young age was the loss of control over her own life. People often made decisions for her, whether it was about what she wore, how she should act, or how she should appear in the media. Nadia was no longer making choices for herself. She was constantly aware of the people around her—fans, reporters, sponsors—who all had their ideas about what she should do next. This constant pressure was a challenge, especially for a young girl who had spent most of her life focused solely on gymnastics. Despite the difficulties, Nadia found ways to stay grounded. She remained close to her family and trusted her coach, Bela Karolyi. They kept her focused on what mattered most:

gymnastics. Even though she was famous, they reminded her that she was still a young gymnast with much to achieve. She didn't let the fame distract her from her passion for gymnastics, and she worked hard to continue improving her routines and performances. Over time, Nadia learned to cope with the fame in her way. She understood it was part of her life now, but she never let it define her. Even as the world changed, Nadia remained dedicated to her sport, constantly striving for excellence. She showed the world that being a young champion and handling fame with grace and dignity was possible. And while the fame was sometimes overwhelming, Nadia's love for gymnastics never wavered. She continued to compete, inspiring millions of young athletes worldwide to pursue their dreams, just as she had.

Balancing School and Gymnastics

As Nadia Comăneci's fame grew, so did her responsibilities. At just 14 years old, she was not only an Olympic champion but also a student, trying to balance the rigorous demands of gymnastics with the typical challenges of school life. It was a tricky balancing act that many young athletes face—juggling academic responsibilities with the intense training schedules required for top-level competition. Before the 1976 Olympics, Nadia's life was primarily about gymnastics. Her days were filled with training at the gym, and her nights were spent resting for the next day's practice. But after her success in Montreal, things changed. Nadia's life was no longer just about perfecting her routines; she now had a full schedule of media appearances, photo shoots, and interviews. While these were exciting opportunities for a young champion, they also took time away from school and gymnastics.

At first, balancing these two worlds was overwhelming. Nadia had to keep up with her studies while training and travelling worldwide. School was important to her, and she wanted to stay caught up, but gymnastics became her passion and priority. She knew that if she wanted to continue to succeed in the sport, she would need to find a way to make both work. Thankfully, her family and coach, Bela Karolyi, were there to support her. They worked together to ensure Nadia could continue her education while pursuing her gymnastics career. Nadia often studied between training sessions, taking schoolwork wherever she went. Whether travelling for competitions or staying home, she found pockets of time to focus on her studies. But it wasn't easy. The long hours in the gym left little time for anything else, and Nadia had to be disciplined to keep up with her lessons. Her studies sometimes took a backseat to her gymnastics commitments, especially when she had to attend events or compete in various countries. During these times, Nadia would rely on tutors to help her stay on track with her schoolwork. The pressure to perform in school and gymnastics was a lot for a young teenager to handle. There were moments when she felt exhausted, torn between her love for gymnastics and her need to succeed in school.

However, Nadia's determination to be both a champion gymnast and a good student motivated her. She knew that education was important for her future, and she didn't want to let her academic dreams slip away while chasing her athletic goals. She was careful to maintain a balance, taking breaks when needed and spending time with her family, who were always there to encourage her. One of the ways Nadia managed her schoolwork was by finding ways to make learning more fun. Her parents and tutors worked with her to make subjects more interesting, often relating them to her gymnastics experience. For example, she would apply the discipline and focus required in gymnastics to her studies. Nadia began to see learning not as a burden but as something that could help her grow inside and outside the gym. Her ability to focus on her academics and her sport helped her succeed in ways many young athletes couldn't. Despite the challenges, Nadia's ability to juggle her academic life with gymnastics showed her incredible work ethic and determination. While many athletes might have been tempted to focus solely on their sport, Nadia understood that balance was crucial to her success. She believed that to be the best gymnast she could be, she also had to be a well-rounded person. She wanted the knowledge and skills that would serve her for a lifetime beyond her gymnastics career. The balancing act was never easy; it sometimes seemed too much. There were days when she felt overwhelmed by the pressure of performing excellently in gymnastics while keeping up with school assignments. But with the help of her family and coach, Nadia learned how to manage both worlds. The skills she developed in

time management, and focus
helped her become a successful
gymnast and a young person
capable of handling multiple
responsibilities. Through this
period of her life, Nadia learned
valuable lessons about balance,
responsibility, and discipline.
These lessons would serve her not
only in gymnastics but also in the
years to come. While her focus was
on gymnastics during her younger
years, Nadia's ability to balance
school and sport showed the world
that young athletes could be
successful in more ways than one.
It was not just about winning gold
medals or breaking records—it was
about growing, learning to manage

different parts of life, and striving
to be the best in all areas.

CHAPTER 5: THE CHALLENGES OF SUCCESS

Facing Pressure and Expectations

After Nadia Comăneci made history at the 1976 Montreal Olympics, her life changed dramatically. No longer just a talented gymnast from Romania, she had become an international icon. As a result, Nadia faced a wave of pressure and high expectations that many young people could never imagine. The attention from the world was both exciting and overwhelming, as people expected her to keep winning, keep achieving, and keep breaking records. This intense pressure was something Nadia had to learn to handle throughout her career. Before the Olympics, Nadia's life had been focused mostly on gymnastics and training. She trained for hours daily, pushing her body to the limit to be the best she could be. She knew what was expected of her at competitions, but the world didn't know her yet. After her success in Montreal, that all changed. The world's attention was now fully on her, bringing rewards and challenges. The constant pressure was one of the hardest parts of achieving such great success at a young age. Nadia was only 14 when she earned her perfect ten score, and soon after, she was the centre of attention. She became a symbol of excellence in gymnastics, and with that came the expectation that she would continue to perform perfectly every time she stepped onto the mat. The pressure to live up to that expectation weighed heavily on her. For a young teenager, the responsibility of being the best in the world was immense. In gymnastics, a sport that values precision, strength, and grace, every move is carefully watched, analyzed, and judged. Nadia knew that if she made even the smallest mistake, everyone would notice it was sure to be flawless, which was always in the back of her mind, and she had to work hard to manage it. As the months passed after the Olympics, Nadia travelled the world for competitions, public appearances, and endorsement deals. She was in the spotlight almost constantly, meaning the world watched every time she competed. Critics were ready to point out her mistakes if she did not perform as expected. The fear of disappointing her fans, coaches, and herself was constant and sometimes overwhelming. While travelling the world and meeting new people was thrilling, Nadia had to sacrifice much of her personal life. She spent less time with her family and friends, and her days were filled with appearances, interviews, and training. The world saw her as a young champion, but behind the scenes, Nadia struggled to balance her desires with the expectations placed upon her. She loved gymnastics, but she also wanted to have a normal childhood. At times, it felt like she was living in a bubble where the world's view of her was more important than hers. In addition to the pressure of performing, Nadia faced scrutiny from the media and the public. Reporters were quick to judge her every move, not only as an athlete but also as a person. They wanted to know everything about her life, thoughts, and feelings. At such a young age, dealing with the constant attention from the media could be exhausting. Nadia had to learn how to block out distractions and stay focused on what was important: her gymnastics. It wasn't easy, but she found strength in her love for the sport and the support of her coach, Bela Karolyi. Another challenge was the physical toll gymnastics took on Nadia's body. The intense training and high-pressure performances left her physically exhausted. Gymnastics is one of the most demanding sports, requiring athletes to use almost every muscle in their body while executing difficult routines. Nadia's body had to be in top shape constantly, and even the slightest injury could cause her to lose points or miss a competition. At times, her body ached, and the strain of training and competing at such a high level became hard to bear. But Nadia was determined not to let her body show signs of weakness. She pushed through the pain, hoping her injuries wouldn't affect her performance. Their expectations of Nadia were not only from the outside world but also from within. She expected herself to continue to be perfect.

Nadia was her own toughest critic. After every routine, she would analyze her performance, wondering if she could have done something better. Even when she earned high scores, she was only sometimes satisfied. Nadia set high standards for herself, which often became more difficult to meet as time passed. Despite all the challenges, Nadia found ways to cope with the pressure. One of the biggest factors in her success was her coach, Bela Karolyi. He was a great coach and mentor, guiding her through difficult times and helping her manage the stress of being a young champion. Bela was always there to reassure her, reminding her of the hard work she had put in and helping her to stay focused on her goals. He taught her how to deal with setbacks and bounce back after disappointments. His belief in her abilities helped Nadia remain positive and motivated, even when things seemed overwhelming. Nadia also learned the importance of taking breaks and finding moments to relax. While gymnastics was her passion, she knew that to be at her best, she needed to rest and recharge. She spent time with her family and friends whenever she could, enjoying life's simple pleasures. This helped her keep perspective and reminded her that while gymnastics was important, it wasn't the only thing that defined her.

Injuries and Setbacks

Despite Nadia Comăneci's remarkable success and the history she made in the 1976 Olympics, the journey to greatness was not without its share of obstacles. As the pressure to be perfect mounted, Nadia also faced physical challenges that tested her resilience and determination. Injuries became a constant concern in her career, and overcoming these setbacks was just as important as achieving success in competitions. Gymnastics is a physically demanding sport. Athletes push their bodies to the limit, performing routines that require flexibility, strength, and precision. While Nadia's natural talent and rigorous training allowed her to perform at an extraordinary level, her body, like all athletes, was not invincible. After the Montreal Olympics, as the expectations for her continued to grow, so did the physical toll gymnastics took on her. One of the most significant challenges Nadia faced was the risk of injury. Gymnasts must perform complex routines on apparatuses such as the balance beam, uneven bars, floor, and vault. The constant high-impact movements, flips, and landings put immense strain on their joints and muscles. Nadia experienced many injuries throughout her career, and some of them threatened to derail her path to success. Her first major injury came just a few years after the 1976 Olympics. In 1977, Nadia suffered an ankle injury while training. This injury was a major setback for her, keeping her out of competition for a while. Ankle injuries are particularly challenging for gymnasts, as they directly affect their ability to perform routines that involve jumping, landing, and balance. Nadia's injury required rest, rehabilitation, and careful management to avoid further damage. It was a reminder that despite her success, she was still vulnerable to the physical demands of the sport. While recovering from her injury, Nadia continued to train, but the fear of re-injury was always in her mind. She knew that every move she made had the potential to cause harm, but she also understood the importance of pushing through the pain. Gymnasts are known for their ability to perform despite being injured, and Nadia was no different. However, this mindset sometimes led her to ignore the warning signs of her body, which could have made her injuries worse in the long run. Nadia's determination to return to competition as quickly as possible sometimes made it difficult to heal fully. She pushed herself harder and harder, often competing through pain. This drive to succeed, while admirable, made it harder for her to recover fully from injuries. She felt the weight of her responsibilities to her fans, coaches, and country, and the idea of letting them down was something she could not bear. As a result, she often sacrificed her well-being to pursue her goals. In

1978, Nadia faced another serious setback. She tore a ligament in her knee during training. This injury was particularly challenging because it required surgery and a long period of rehabilitation. A knee injury for a gymnast is one of the most difficult setbacks because it affects the ability to jump, land, and perform other essential movements. Nadia's recovery process was slow; she had to focus on regaining her strength and flexibility. This period of rest and healing was incredibly frustrating for a young athlete who had known only the intensity of constant competition and training. During her recovery, Nadia had to learn patience. She was used to pushing herself to the limit, but now she had to accept that her body needed time to heal. The physical therapy was gruelling, and Nadia spent hours strengthening her knee and improving her flexibility daily. She had to regain her confidence in performing the routines that had once come so easily to her. It was a mental challenge as much as a physical one, but with the support of her coach, Bela Karolyi, and her family, Nadia slowly began to heal. The recovery process taught Nadia an important lesson about self-care. As a young gymnast, she had been focused solely on achieving her goals, often at the expense of her body's needs. Now, she understood that success was about pushing through the pain and caring for herself to perform at her best. This shift in perspective was important not just for her career but also for her long-term well-being. Despite the challenges, Nadia made a remarkable comeback. She returned to competition in 1979, but the path back to her previous level of performance took work. She had to rebuild her strength, refine her skills, and regain the confidence that had made her a champion. Nadia's comeback was a testament to her perseverance,

determination, and ability to
bounce back from setbacks. Each
time she faced a challenge, she met
it head-on, refusing to let injuries
define her or stop her from
pursuing her dreams. In addition
to the physical setbacks, Nadia
also had to deal with the mental
toll that injuries took on her. Every
time she injured herself, she had to
confront the fear of not being able
to compete again at the highest
level. The thought of losing her
place in the sport she loved was
terrifying, and the pressure to
recover quickly only added to the
stress. Yet, through each injury,
Nadia proved to herself that she
could overcome anything that

came her way. The mental strength she developed through these setbacks made her even more resilient and prepared her for the challenges that would come in the future.

CHAPTER 6: THE ROAD TO THE 1980 OLYMPICS

Training for Another Gold

After the incredible success of the 1976 Olympics, Nadia Comăneci had proven herself as one of the greatest gymnasts the world had ever seen. She became an icon, inspiring athletes worldwide with her perfect 10s and graceful routines. However, Nadia's journey didn't end in Montreal. The world was watching, and the pressure to continue performing at the highest level was immense. As the 1980 Olympics in Moscow approached, Nadia knew she had a great challenge ahead of her. She was determined to defend her Olympic title and earn another gold medal. But the road to the 1980 Olympics was not an easy one. Training for another gold medal was different from the first time. In 1976, Nadia had been young, full of energy, and relatively unknown on the world stage. By 1980, she had become a star. The expectations were higher, and the competition had grown tougher. Nadia was no longer just a young gymnast with potential—she was a champion who had to prove she could stay on top. To prepare for the 1980 Olympics, Nadia's training became more intense and focused. Her coach, Bela Karolyi, had always pushed her to be the best, but now the stakes were even higher. The routines were harder, the expectations more demanding, and the pressure to perform perfectly was overwhelming. Training for another Olympic gold would require dedication, hard work, and, most importantly, overcoming the physical and mental challenges of being a champion. One of the key aspects of Nadia's training was refining her skills on the four gymnastics apparatuses: the balance beam, uneven bars, vault, and floor exercise. Each event required different skills and techniques, and Nadia had to perfect every movement. She spent hours every day working on her routines, ensuring that every jump, twist, and flip was as close to flawless as possible. Even the smallest mistake could cost her a perfect score, so every detail mattered. Nadia's commitment to perfection was evident in her countless hours in the gym, practising until her body ached. Despite her success, Nadia still faced physical challenges. She had already endured injuries earlier in her career, and the years of training had taken a toll on her body. Her muscles were sore, and her joints often ached from the constant strain of gymnastics. Yet, Nadia was determined not to let these physical setbacks get her way. She knew that to compete at the highest level, she had to endure the pain and keep training. The road to the 1980 Olympics was about mastering new skills and maintaining the strength and endurance necessary to perform at an elite level. In addition to physical training, Nadia had to work on her mental game. As a young champion, the pressure to perform at the same level as she did in 1976 was overwhelming. The world watched her every move, and there was a constant fear of failure. Nadia had to learn to block distractions and focus solely on her performance. The pressure to win another gold medal was intense, but she had to stay calm and confident. She had already made history once and had to prove to herself and the world that she could do it again. Nadia's mental preparation was just as important as her physical training. She worked with her coach, Bela Karolyi, to develop strategies for staying focused and confident during competition. Karolyi knew how important it was to help Nadia manage the pressure, and he worked with her to build mental resilience. They focused on techniques like visualization and

positive thinking, which helped
Nadia stay calm and focused in the
face of intense pressure. She had
to believe in herself, trust in her
training, and remember that she
was capable of greatness. As the
1980 Olympics drew closer, Nadia
began to feel the weight of
expectations. The world had seen
her achieve perfection once
before, and now she was expected
to do it again. But this time, the
pressure was even greater. She was
no longer the unknown young
gymnast who stunned the world
with a perfect 10—she was a world
champion with a target on her
back. Nadia knew the competition
would be fierce, and other

gymnasts also aimed for the gold. But despite the pressure, she refused to let it shake her resolve. Training for another gold was about physical preparation and dealing with the mental and emotional challenges of being a top athlete. Nadia had already reached the pinnacle of her sport, and the desire to stay there was strong. She was motivated by the dream of winning another gold medal and the desire to prove to herself and the world that her first victory was not a fluke. She had to show that she was more than just a one-time wonder—she was a true champion who could compete and win at the highest level year after year. As the days leading up to the 1980 Olympics ticked away, Nadia's training became more focused. Every moment in the gym was critical, and there was little room for error. But despite the demanding schedule, Nadia's passion for gymnastics never wavered. She loved the sport and was determined to continue making history. Her training for the 1980 Olympics was a testament to her unwavering commitment, desire to succeed, and belief in her abilities. By the time the Olympics finally arrived, Nadia was ready. She had spent years training, pushing her body to its limits, and learning to stay mentally strong under pressure. Nadia knew that winning another gold medal would require everything she had—her strength, skills, and mental toughness—but she was ready to face the challenge head-on.

Competing in Moscow

The 1980 Olympic Games in Moscow were unlike any competition Nadia Comăneci had ever experienced. Expectations were higher after the incredible triumph of the 1976 Olympics, where she became the first gymnast to score a perfect 10. The world watched her every move, waiting to see if she could repeat her past success. Nadia was no longer just a young gymnast—she was a legend in the making, and competing in Moscow was her chance to prove that she could maintain her place at the top of the gymnastics world. The competition in Moscow was fierce, with some of the best gymnasts worldwide aiming for gold. Nadia knew she would face tough rivals, but her experience from the 1976 Olympics gave her confidence. She had faced high expectations before and had risen to the challenge, and she was determined to do the same in 1980. However, there was more pressure now. She wasn't just a rising star; she was already a champion, and the world wanted to see if she could defend her title. When Nadia arrived in Moscow, the atmosphere was electric. The Olympic Games were always grand, but the gymnastics competition, in particular, was intense. Nadia had prepared for this moment for years, and now it was time to perform on the world stage again. She knew that to win, she would have to push herself to new limits—physically, mentally, and emotionally. The gymnastics competition began, and Nadia's first event was the vault. The vault had always been one of her strong suits, and she was determined to start strong. Her routine was flawless, and she received high marks from the judges. Nadia felt a surge of confidence as she moved on to the next event, the uneven bars. This was one of her most challenging events, but Nadia had worked tirelessly to perfect her routine. She executed every movement with precision and grace, again earning high marks. As the competition continued, Nadia's composure and focus were evident. She was determined to show the world that she could maintain her level of excellence. With each passing routine, Nadia's confidence grew. Her ability to perform under pressure set her apart from many other gymnasts.

She was no longer just competing against her rivals—she was competing against her expectations, striving to maintain the perfection she had achieved in 1976. But it wasn't just about perfection—it was also about consistency. Nadia knew every movement counted, and any mistake could cost her the gold medal. The balance beam was next, one of the most difficult events in gymnastics. She was balancing on the beam, which required strength, skill, and a deep mental focus. Nadia had struggled with the balance beam but worked tirelessly to improve. As she stepped onto the beam, she took a deep breath and reminded herself of all the hours of training that had prepared her for this moment. Nadia performed a flawless routine, earning one of the day's highest scores. With one event left—the floor exercise—Nadia knew she was close to achieving her goal. The floor exercise was her favourite event, where she could show off her creativity and express herself through dance and movement. This was her opportunity to shine, to give the audience a performance they would remember. As she danced and tumbled across the floor, the crowd was captivated by her energy and precision. Nadia's routine was filled with strength and elegance, and she finished with a powerful leap that left the audience in awe. Once again, the judges rewarded her with high marks. By the end of the competition, Nadia had proven herself once again as one of the greatest gymnasts in the world. She had competed with grace, skill, and poise and maintained her composure throughout the intense pressure of the Olympic Games. Her performances were extraordinary, and she was rewarded with several gold medals. But the journey to the 1980 Olympics was about more than just winning gold. It was about

proving to herself and the world
that she was still a champion,
capable of achieving greatness.
Nadia's victory in Moscow was a
testament to her perseverance,
dedication, and ability to handle
the immense pressure of being one
of the most famous athletes in the
world. For Nadia, the competition
in Moscow was not just about
winning—it was about showing the
world that she was more than just
the gymnast who had earned the
first perfect 10. She was a
champion who could continue to
excel even when the pressure was
at its peak. Her victory in 1980
solidified her place in gymnastics
history, and her journey was a

shining example of what it took to succeed at the highest level. As the 1980 Olympics ended, Nadia's legacy was firmly cemented. She had proven that her 1976 triumph was not a fluke and showed the world that she could handle the pressure and competition of the highest level. Nadia's success in Moscow culminated years of hard work, dedication, and passion for the sport. It was a reminder that success is not just about winning—it's about perseverance, commitment, and the willingness to keep pushing forward, no matter the obstacles.

CHAPTER 7: LIFE BEYOND COMPETITIVE GYMNASTICS

Leaving Competitive Gymnastics

After years of dominating the world of gymnastics, Nadia Comăneci's time as a competitive gymnast eventually ended. Her decision to step away from the sport was not an easy one. Having captured the world's attention with her perfect 10s and Olympic gold medals, Nadia had been one of the most recognized athletes in the world. But as the years passed, the pressures of constant competition and the toll it took on her body and mind became too much to ignore. At just 20 years old, she left competitive gymnastics and moved on to the next chapter of her life. Mixed emotions marked Nadia's departure from gymnastics. On one hand, she was grateful for the incredible experiences the sport had given her and proud of everything she had achieved. On the other hand, leaving the sport she loved was bittersweet. Gymnastics had been a huge part of her life since she was a little girl, and it was hard to imagine life without it. But as she looked toward the future, Nadia knew that there was more to life than gymnastics, and she was ready to explore what that future could hold. Leaving competitive gymnastics meant adjusting to a new lifestyle. For years, Nadia had been part of a rigorous training schedule, constantly pushing herself to perform at her best. Now, without the daily demands of training, she could explore other interests and passions. She no longer had to wake up early for practice or spend hours perfecting routines. Instead, she could focus on different aspects of her life—things she had put on hold while pursuing her gymnastics career. Despite leaving the gym, Nadia's fame and success followed her wherever she went. She became a global icon, admired for her accomplishments and how she revolutionized the sport. Her perfect ten had changed gymnastics forever, and she remained a beloved figure in the sports world. However, the attention she received also came with challenges. It was easier for Nadia to move forward by constantly being reminded of her past achievements. People still saw her as a young gymnast who made history, and it wasn't always easy for her to carve out a new identity beyond that. As she began life outside gymnastics, Nadia focused on her personal life and relationships. She moved to the

United States and started to
experience life completely
differently. She was no longer just
a gymnast but a young woman
exploring new opportunities.
Nadia eventually married
Romanian gymnast Bart Conner,
another Olympic gold medalist,
and they started a family together.
This latest chapter in her life was
focused on building a family,
enjoying her relationships, and
finding new ways to stay
connected to the sport she once
loved. Nadia also became involved
in various charitable and
humanitarian efforts. Throughout
her career, she had been aware of
her platform and the responsibility

that came with it. Now that she had more time to focus on causes close to her heart, she used her influence to support children's programs, health initiatives, and gymnastics organizations. She found fulfilment in giving back to the community and helping others. Her charity work allowed her to continue positively impacting the world despite her no longer competing. While it was clear that gymnastics would always be a part of Nadia's life, her focus shifted away from competition and to other pursuits. She started to explore new opportunities, including becoming a commentator and ambassador for the sport. Nadia's insights into gymnastics and personal experience made her a respected voice in the sport. She used this platform to help promote gymnastics and inspire young athletes who dreamed of one day achieving the same level of success that she had. Despite her new life outside of gymnastics, Nadia continued to stay connected to the sport that had brought her so much fame. She supported young gymnasts and attended competitions, offering her encouragement and expertise. Her presence at these events was a reminder of her incredible legacy, and her influence on the sport remained strong even after her competitive career had ended. Nadia also found new ways to inspire the next generation of gymnasts. She was often invited to speak at schools and events, where she shared her story and encouraged young people to follow their dreams, no matter the obstacles they might face. Her journey from a young gymnast in Romania to an Olympic legend was one of perseverance and determination, and she used her story to motivate others to push through challenges and never give up. While the years following her retirement were filled with change and new experiences, Nadia

Comăneci never forgot the lessons gymnastics had taught her. The discipline, the drive, and the belief in herself that she had gained from her years of training and competition stayed with her throughout her life. These qualities shaped her in everything she did, whether in her relationships, charitable work, or ongoing connection to gymnastics.

Finding New Passions

After leaving competitive gymnastics, Nadia Comăneci faced the challenge of reinventing herself. The world had come to know her as the young gymnast who had achieved the impossible, but Nadia was determined to prove that she was more than just her achievements in the gym. Although she had achieved legendary status in gymnastics, Nadia was eager to explore new paths, find new passions, and experience life beyond the world of competition. Nadia quickly realized that her journey did not end with her retirement from gymnastics. She had spent so many years training and competing that she had little time to explore the world beyond the gym. Now that she could do so, she embraced it fully. One of the first things she discovered was a deep interest in helping others.

Throughout her career, she had always been aware of the platform that her fame had given her. Now, she uses this platform to give back to the community and support important causes. One of Nadia's new passions became advocating for children's health and well-being. During her time in the spotlight, she had seen firsthand the positive impact that sports and physical activity could have on young people's lives. Now, she used her influence to promote the importance of staying active and healthy, encouraging children to pursue sports and lead healthy lifestyles. Nadia's involvement in children's programs allowed her to

combine her love for athletics with
her desire to make a difference in
the lives of young people. As part
of her commitment to giving back,
Nadia became involved with the
Special Olympics, an organization
that provides sports opportunities
for children and adults with
intellectual disabilities. This cause
resonated with her deeply, and she
dedicated much of her time to
supporting the organization and
raising awareness about the
importance of inclusion and equal
opportunities for all athletes,
regardless of their abilities.
Through her work with the Special
Olympics, Nadia discovered a new
passion for advocacy and social

causes. In addition to her work with charities and organizations, Nadia also found joy in exploring new hobbies and interests that she hadn't had time for while competing. One of the things she enjoyed most was travel. As a gymnast, her travel was often limited to competitions, but now, she could explore the world at her own pace. Nadia travelled to many countries, experiencing new cultures and making lasting memories. Her travels allowed her to broaden her horizons and discover a world beyond gymnastics. Nadia also explored her creative side by dabbling in various forms of art. She had

always been fascinated by the
world of design and aesthetics,
and now she could explore these
interests. She began
experimenting with interior design
and home decor, finding
satisfaction in creating beautiful
and functional spaces. Her passion
for design grew over time, and she
became more involved in projects
that allowed her to express her
creativity. Nadia also enjoyed
painting and drawing, using art to
relax and unwind. These creative
outlets gave her a sense of
fulfilment and joy outside the gym.
As she settled into her new life,
Nadia also found that her
connection to gymnastics was far

from over. She might have stepped away from competitive gymnastics, but her love for the sport never waned. Instead of competing, Nadia shifted her focus to sharing her knowledge and passion for gymnastics with others. She became a mentor and coach, working with young gymnasts who looked up to her as a role model. Nadia enjoyed helping young athletes develop their skills and encouraging them to reach their full potential. Her experience and expertise made her a valuable resource for those starting the sport. In addition to mentoring, Nadia continued to support gymnastics in other ways.

She became an ambassador for the sport, representing gymnastics at international events and promoting its benefits to a wider audience. Nadia also attended gymnastics competitions and offered her insights and feedback to athletes and coaches. Her presence at these events served as a reminder of her legacy and her deep love for the sport that had shaped her life. As Nadia's life evolved, she also found happiness in her relationships. She married American gymnast Bart Conner, and they became one of the most famous power couples in gymnastics. Their shared experiences in the sport created a strong bond, and they supported each other as they navigated life outside of competitive gymnastics. Together, they co-founded the Bart Conner Gymnastics Academy, where they helped train the next generation of gymnasts. This new chapter in their lives allowed them to work together, combining their passion for the sport with their desire to give back to the gymnastics community. Nadia's passion for giving back extended to the development of gymnastics in her home country, Romania. She worked with various organizations and initiatives to help improve the sport in Romania and support the development of young athletes.

Her contributions to gymnastics went beyond her career, and she became a key figure in the global gymnastics community, advocating for the growth and improvement of the sport worldwide.

CHAPTER 8: BECOMING A GLOBAL INSPIRATION

Mentoring Young Gymnasts

After Nadia Comăneci's extraordinary success in gymnastics, she became more than just a world champion—a symbol of dedication, perseverance, and achievement. Known for her perfect 10 in the 1976 Montreal Olympics, Nadia's accomplishments were unmatched, and her influence continued to grow long after her competitive career had ended. As she navigated life after gymnastics, mentoring young gymnasts was one of the most important roles she embraced. This was a way for her to pass on her lessons and help shape the future of the sport she loved. Becoming a mentor was a natural step for Nadia, who had always believed in the power of discipline, hard work, and self-belief. These values were at the core of her success, and she knew that by sharing them with the next generation, she could help others reach their dreams. With her experience and fame, Nadia was uniquely positioned to guide aspiring gymnasts, providing them with technical advice and emotional support. She became a role model, someone they could look up to and trust as they navigated the challenges of gymnastics. Nadia's approach to mentoring was deeply personal and involved much more than simply teaching skills and techniques. She understood the pressure young gymnasts face, and she made it a point to connect with them on an emotional level. Many of the young athletes she mentored faced the same intense expectations and challenges she had encountered during her career. Nadia knew what it felt like to be under constant pressure to perform, and she wanted to help gymnasts balance their passion for the sport with their mental and emotional well-being. As a mentor, Nadia provided guidance in training and dealing with the ups and downs of being an elite athlete. She shared her experiences of overcoming obstacles, managing stress, and coping with setbacks. She wanted to make sure that the young gymnasts she worked with knew that it was okay to face difficulties and that perseverance was the key to overcoming them. Her words and actions taught them that success wasn't just about winning medals—it was about enjoying the journey, improving every day, and never giving up, no matter how hard the road ahead might seem. Her mentorship extended to young gymnasts in the United States and worldwide. Nadia's fame earned her international recognition, and her involvement in various gymnastics organizations allowed her to work with athletes from different countries and cultures. She travelled extensively, visiting gymnastics academies and speaking at events where she could offer advice and encouragement to young gymnasts who dreamed of one day reaching the same heights she had. She became a source of inspiration for those who admired her past accomplishments and saw her as a symbol of strength and resilience. Through her work with young gymnasts, Nadia emphasized the importance of setting goals and staying focused on the long-term vision. Gymnastics is a sport that requires years of dedication and hard work, and Nadia understood that success doesn't come overnight. She encouraged athletes to set short-term and long-term goals, stay motivated even when progress felt slow, and trust in their ability to achieve great things over time. She taught them that every small step toward improvement was worth celebrating and that they should always maintain their dreams, even if the journey is challenging. Nadia also advocated for the importance of balance in a gymnast's life. In her career, she had experienced the intense pressure of competition, and she knew that the best athletes could maintain a healthy balance between training and personal life. As a mentor, she urged young gymnasts to make time for school, family, and friendships and to take care of their physical and mental health. She explained that enjoying life outside of gymnastics was important, as this would make them better athletes and happier, well-rounded individuals. Her advice was invaluable to young gymnasts who were sometimes consumed by the demanding nature of their sport. In addition to her one-on-one mentoring, Nadia worked to create opportunities for young gymnasts to learn from her expertise on a larger scale. She helped organize gymnastics camps, clinics, and workshops where aspiring athletes could receive top-level coaching and guidance. At these events, Nadia would demonstrate her signature skills, provide training tips, and offer motivational talks encouraging gymnasts to stay committed to their craft. These camps and clinics also allowed young athletes to connect, share

their experiences, and build a
community of support. Nadia's
legacy as a mentor extended
beyond just the technical side of
gymnastics. She believed that the
mental and emotional aspects of
the sport were just as important as
physical training. She emphasized
the importance of staying positive,
managing nerves, and maintaining
confidence, especially when faced
with challenges. Through her
mentorship, young gymnasts
learned that it wasn't just their
athletic ability that would
determine their success—their
mindset, determination, and
willingness to keep going even
when things got tough. Her

mentoring efforts were not only about helping gymnasts become better athletes; they were about helping them become better people. Nadia believed that gymnastics could teach valuable life lessons, such as perseverance, resilience, and the importance of hard work. She wanted young gymnasts to leave the sport, knowing they had grown as athletes and individuals. The athletes who had the privilege of learning from her were not just trained in gymnastics—they were equipped with the tools they needed to succeed in all aspects of life. In many ways, Nadia's work as a mentor was a reflection of her journey. She had faced immense pressure, struggled with injuries, and dealt with the challenges of being a young athlete in the spotlight. By mentoring young gymnasts, Nadia could pass on the wisdom and insights she had gained from her own experiences, helping the next generation of athletes avoid some of the pitfalls she had encountered. She taught them how to be better gymnasts and people—strong, confident, and capable of handling whatever life threw their way.

Promoting the Sport Worldwide

After Nadia Comăneci's historic achievements in gymnastics, her fame spread far beyond the borders of Romania, reaching corners of the globe where gymnastics had previously been a lesser-known sport. Her perfect 10s at the 1976 Montreal Olympics became an international sensation, captivating millions and sparking a newfound interest in gymnastics worldwide. As Nadia became a global icon, she used her platform to promote the sport in her home country and internationally. Her dedication to expanding the sport's reach and inspiring future generations of athletes became one of her most enduring contributions. Nadia recognized that her unique position as the first gymnast to achieve a perfect 10 in an Olympic competition made her an influential figure in the world of sports. With this recognition came an opportunity to give back to gymnastics and help it grow internationally. She travelled extensively, visiting gymnastics academies, speaking at international events, and appearing in media outlets worldwide. Her charisma, accomplishments, and passion for the sport made her an ideal ambassador for gymnastics, and she used every opportunity to advocate for the sport's inclusion in schools, local clubs, and international competitions. Through her travels, Nadia worked to raise the profile of gymnastics in countries where the sport had yet to reach its full potential. In many places, gymnastics was seen as a niche or elite activity practised by a small group of athletes. Nadia's visibility helped to shift this perception. Her appearance at major gymnastics events worldwide drew attention to the sport, inspiring young athletes to take up gymnastics. In addition to promoting the sport, she emphasized the importance of physical fitness and discipline, showing that gymnastics could help build strength, coordination, and flexibility for athletes of all backgrounds and ages. One of Nadia's key goals was to make gymnastics more accessible to children. She understood that many young athletes, especially those from disadvantaged backgrounds, did not have the resources or opportunities to pursue gymnastics at a high level. To address this, she worked with gymnastics federations and schools to create programs to bring the sport to a wider audience. Nadia's efforts were focused on ensuring that the joy and benefits of gymnastics were available to anyone, regardless of their economic status or geographical location. As a global ambassador, Nadia also worked to improve the infrastructure and coaching systems in many countries. She often collaborated with gymnastics organizations, helping to improve training programs and facilities for young gymnasts. By working with coaches and athletes worldwide, Nadia shared the lessons she had learned from her own experience and helped raise the standard of gymnastics worldwide. Her influence was particularly evident in Eastern Europe, where her fame had already created a strong following. Still, she also made significant strides in countries where gymnastics was beginning to grow in popularity. Nadia also advocated for the development of women's gymnastics on a global scale. Women's gymnastics was still evolving at the time of her Olympic success, and many countries still needed to embrace it fully. Nadia's perfect ten at the Montreal Olympics helped to break down barriers for female athletes, showing that women could achieve greatness in sports traditionally dominated by men. Her success encouraged countless young girls to pursue gymnastics and believe that they, too, could excel. Nadia's advocacy for women's sports extended beyond gymnastics. She became a vocal supporter of women's rights in athletics, encouraging more girls and women to participate in all sports, not just gymnastics. Through her involvement in promoting the sport, Nadia helped establish the importance of international competitions and events. She recognized that competitions like the World Championships, the World Cup, and the Olympics were essential for the growth of gymnastics. Nadia supported these events, attending them whenever she

could, and used them as platforms
to bring attention to the sport. She
emphasized that these events were
not just opportunities for
gymnasts to showcase their skills
but also for fans and supporters to
appreciate the beauty and artistry
of gymnastics. Nadia's
commitment to promoting
gymnastics also extended into the
realm of media. She appeared in
commercials, television shows,
and documentaries, using her fame
to raise awareness about
gymnastics. She became the face
of several gymnastics-related
products and brands, which
helped fund programs to increase
access to the sport. Her public

appearances were about
enhancing her career and
spreading the message that
gymnastics was a sport for
everyone, regardless of
background. They could bring joy,
confidence, and life lessons to
those practising it. One of the most
lasting impacts of Nadia's
promotion of gymnastics
worldwide was her inspiration to
young athletes. Through her global
outreach, she reached thousands
of children, encouraging them to
pursue their dreams in gymnastics.
Her story became a beacon of hope
and possibility, showing young
gymnasts they could achieve
greatness just like she did with

determination, hard work, and a love for the sport. Nadia's legacy as a promoter of gymnastics was not just about winning medals or setting records—it was about creating opportunities for others to follow in her footsteps. In addition to inspiring young athletes, Nadia worked to bring gymnastics to the forefront of the global sports community. She believed that gymnastics, combined with strength, flexibility, and grace, was one of the most beautiful sports in the world. She wanted others to see it the way she did—a sport that required skill and athleticism and offered a chance for personal expression and achievement. Through her efforts, gymnastics became more visible, more respected, and more widely practised than ever before. Nadia's role in promoting gymnastics was a testament to her enduring love for the sport. She recognized that her success had paved the way for future generations of gymnasts and took that responsibility seriously. By making gymnastics more accessible, inclusive, and visible worldwide, she ensured that her legacy would live on, inspiring young athletes to follow their dreams and reach for the stars—just as she had done on that

unforgettable day in 1976 when
she earned her perfect 10.

CONCLUSION

Nadia Comăneci's journey from a young girl with a dream in Romania to a global gymnastics icon is more than just a tale of athletic achievement—it's a story of perseverance, determination, and the power of believing in yourself, even when the odds seem impossible. Her groundbreaking achievement of scoring the first perfect 10 in gymnastics at the 1976 Montreal Olympics changed the sport forever. It proved that with hard work, discipline, and dedication, records can be shattered, and limits can be redefined. Nadia's legacy goes far beyond the perfect scores, the medals, and the fame. What makes her truly special is the inspiration she continues to provide to gymnasts, athletes, and dreamers worldwide. Her story teaches us that success is not just about winning or being the best—it's about pushing yourself to be better than you were yesterday and never giving up, no matter how challenging the path may seem. Nadia faced countless obstacles, from the pressures of competition to the difficulties of transitioning from a young champion to a woman in the spotlight. Yet, through it all, she remained grounded, focused on her goals, and committed to her passion for gymnastics. One of the key lessons from Nadia's life is the importance of resilience. She didn't just excel in gymnastics because of her natural talent; she thrived because of her relentless drive to improve and overcome setbacks. When faced with challenges, she didn't back down. Instead, she worked harder, pushed through pain, and refused to let anything stand in her way. This mindset is something that all of us can apply to our own lives—whether in sports, school or any other endeavour. Nadia's example shows us that failure is not the end but a stepping stone on the road to success. It's the ability to get back up after falling and keep going when it feels like you can't which defines a champion. Nadia's impact also goes beyond just those who are involved in gymnastics. Her legacy reminds us that we all have the power to inspire others. Through her story, Nadia showed the world that no dream is too big, no challenge is too difficult, and no barrier is too strong to break through. Whether as gymnasts, educators, or role models, we can make a positive difference in someone else's life. Nadia's career and life encourage us to use our unique talents to inspire others, just as she inspired millions of young athletes to believe in themselves and chase their dreams. As a mentor to young gymnasts and an advocate for the sport, Nadia continues influencing generations of athletes. She has always been dedicated to passing on her knowledge of gymnastics techniques and life lessons about work ethic, humility, and passion. Nadia has demonstrated that greatness is not measured by perfection but by the effort you put into everything you do and the heart you put into the journey. Her willingness to share her wisdom with others ensures that her legacy lives on in today's gymnasts and

tomorrow's stars. Her influence
reaches beyond gymnastics,
teaching us the importance of hard
work, dedication, and the courage
to chase our passions, no matter
what. Nadia's life shows us that
true success is not about medals or
fame—it's about using your
success to help others, to lift them,
and to show them that anything is
possible. Whether you are an
athlete, an artist, a student, or
anyone with a dream, Nadia's story
teaches us that we can achieve
greatness by believing in
ourselves, staying committed to
our goals, and inspiring others. As
we reflect on her journey and the
incredible marks she left on the

world, let us remember that the
spirit of Nadia Comăneci is not just
about the glory of the past but
about the potential of the future.
Her legacy is still alive today,
carried forward by the countless
young athletes who look up to her
and draw strength from her story.
Every time a gymnast steps onto
the mat, every time an athlete
pushes past their limits, they are
continuing the work that Nadia
started in Montreal. Nadia has
shown us that the path to success
is always challenging but
worthwhile. Her life reminds us to
stay focused, to believe in
ourselves, and to never give up on
our dreams, no matter how

difficult they may seem. She has set the bar for all of us, not just in gymnastics but in life, and her example will continue to inspire generations for years to come. So, let Nadia's story be a guiding light for all of us, a reminder that we can all reach for the stars with determination, passion, and hard work. Her journey has shown us that there are no limits to what we can achieve and no dream too big to chase. As Nadia did on that unforgettable day in Montreal, we can make history and inspire the world.

Made in the USA
Columbia, SC
10 February 2025

53663778R00089